Herefordshire Life

Photographs by Derek Evans

Herefordshire Life

Photographs by Derek Evans

COMPILED BY KEITH JAMES

TEMPUS

Frontispiece: Derek Evans, with one of two studio Rolleiflex cameras shortly after opening his first studio on the top floor of No. 41 (later renumbered No. 43) Broad Street.

First published 2005

Tempus Publishing Limited
The Mill, Brimscombe Port,
Stroud, Gloucestershire, GL5 2QG
www.tempus-publishing.com

British Library Cataloguing in Publication Data.
A catalogue record for this book is available from the British Library.

ISBN 0 7524 3724 0

Typesetting and origination by Tempus Publishing Limited.
Printed in Great Britain.

Contents

Acknowledgements

Thanks are due to Mr Graham England for long hours in a summer heatwave matching words to pictures and to Dr Derek Foxton, who offered accurate descriptions of now lost landmarks.

Introduction

For nearly half a century, Hereford photographer Derek Evans FRPS, FRSA has been perhaps the most widely recognised face among the local journalists. Born the son of a Welsh miner, his childhood passion for photography was evident and encouraged by those who saw his talent. In a corner of the darkened projection room at the Ritz cinema, films and prints could be safely developed, under the tutelage of organist Roy Slater – himself a keen photographer.

Following two years' National Service his exceptional career as a freelance photographer began and the year 1951 honoured him with an Associateship of the Royal Photographic Society and later in the same year he became a Fellow of the Royal Society for the Encouragement of Arts. One of the few photographers capable of mastering the delicate and perilous problems of correctly exposing the new but slow colour transparency films, he joined the *National Geographic* team to record the Queen's coronation. Back in Hereford his first studio opened in Broad Street and freelance commissions flowed from local, regional and national papers. With enormous success at international photographic exhibitions his reputation spread to mainland Europe, particularly France and Belgium where he was considered a master of *contre jour* lighting.

By 1960, his studio was at its most prolific and industrious. Newspapers and magazines were flourishing and industry was gripped with a need to communicate to its workforce and its customers. Regional television was set to boom and he quickly recognised the geographical advantage of being almost equidistant between Cardiff and Birmingham. With two 16mm Paillard Bolex clockwork cameras and one standard 16mm Arriflex, short newsreels could be sold on an almost daily basis to TWW (later HTV) at Cardiff and ATV (later Central TV) at Birmingham. Some days a cameraman would be needed on top of the towers of the first Severn Bridge to film the spinning of the cables across the estuary, while on other days the sound of racing fire engines would herald either spectacle or tragedy. And filming for the BBC was not left out of the equation, nor the demands for coverage of weekend sport. Long before the electronic age, with filming complete, 100- or 400-foot spools of film had then to be raced to the studios for processing and transmission for the early evening news bulletins. This workload gifted training to the studio assistants, a privileged introduction to the news editors in television newsrooms and equally to the Fleet Street picture desks. The exceptional reputation of the Broad Street studio opened careers for television cameramen such as Mike Charity, Rik Caulder and Graham Essenhigh. From earlier times John Bulmer would make outstanding contributions to the fledgling *Sunday Times* Colour Supplement while part-timers such as local historian Dr Derek Foxton, then a dental student, would find the studio's creative and addictive work the start of a life-long interest.

Derek Evans started with glass plates and home-made chemicals but in his long career his innate skills comprehensively mastered changing technology. The widespread introduction of colour photography in the mid-1960s, and the move from film to video by the television industry in the early eighties, were simply different tools with which to work. Energetically driving the studio forward and feeding newspapers and television with news and features, the breadth of work was wide ranging. The infectious laughter of personalities such as Harry Secombe and Sammy Davis Jr, the sobriety of State and Royal occasions and tragedies such as the Aberfan School disaster were all disseminated from the studio. And theses productive years were applauded nationally by his peers. In 1966, Derek was elected a Fellow of the Royal Photographic Society and became a founding member of its Photojournalism Group, serving as chairman for a good number of years.

His journalistic curiosity and enthusiasm dipped in and out of Herefordshire life on a daily basis and fed his knowledge of local events or newsworthy items. In 1971, he became Chairman of Hereford Rotary Club while still serving as an elected city councillor but he never neglected his sporting interests. As a young man he was, for a short while, a player with Shrewsbury Town FC and remains a life-long supporter and shareholder of Hereford United FC. Summer evenings were spent playing cricket for Hereford City Sports Club and long hours golfing at home and abroad were sealed with the captaincy of Hereford Golf Club in 1987.

His political sympathies are well known and he was for many years from 1965 an elected Liberal city councillor; firstly for Tupsley ward and later Central. For over forty years he has striven to return a Liberal MP to the seat, after serving as press officer to all the candidates during that period, including the late Sir Robin Day. Elected to the Presidency of Hereford Liberal Association the reward came in 1997 when Paul Keetch won the South Hereford Constituency for the Liberals.

Now retired, his legacy remains in the expertise of those who owe their careers to him and in his library of pictures – a selection of which from the early days are seen in these pages.

Keith James
August, 2005

Foreword

By Paul Keetch MP

There can be few people who can claim to have such an influence on their community as Derek Evans and even fewer who have been able to record it so well. He has been both an extraordinary observer and participant. There is poignancy to the 1958 image of the toddlers paddling in the River Wye next to the Victoria footbridge when the only other site was way across town at the old municipal swimming baths in Edgar Street. It would be nearly twenty years after taking this picture that Derek, as Chairman of the Leisure and Recreation Committee of Hereford City Council, would pull the money together to build the new swimming baths on the King George's Playing Fields for the enjoyment of a whole new generation. And maybe there were other times when Derek witnessed something only to remedy its shortcomings at some more appropriate time.

Having known Derek and campaigned with him virtually all my political life I remember his tears of joy at my first electoral triumph. It is fitting that a wider audience sees this intriguing selection from such an industrious career. These are pictures that reflect this charismatic, vigorous and interesting man – pictures with a sense of well-being, fun and sometimes even mischief.

Paul Keetch MP
House of Commons, August, 2005

At an age when most men would have retired, sixty-five-year-old Jack Pye swung from his boson's chair to repoint the spire of All Saints' church – the city's tallest. Below the steeplejack, traffic moves along Broad Street towards the cathedral.

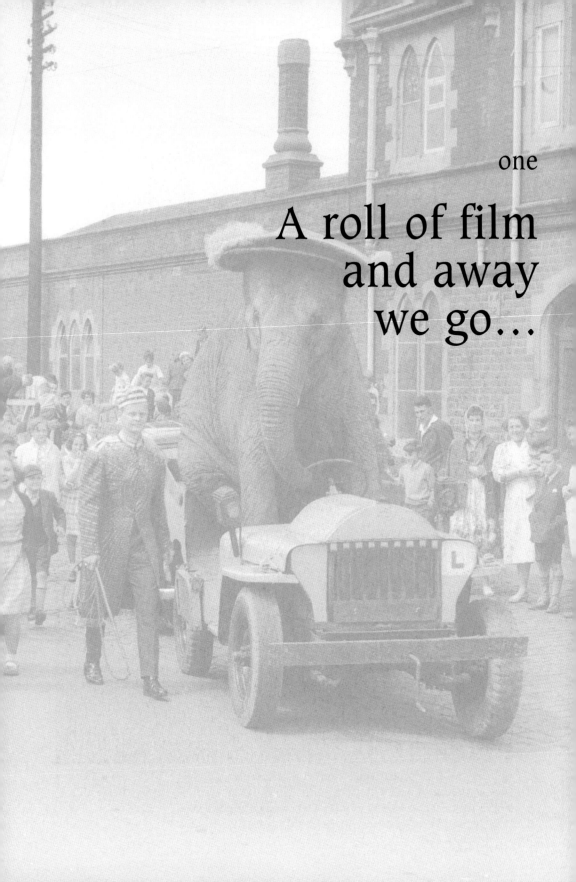

one

A roll of film and away we go...

Children's idol Peter Brough and his ventriloquist dummy, Archie Andrews, added an extra performance to their scheduled shows at the Kemble Theatre when they entertained children on a visit to Holmer School.

Opposite: Almost on Derek Evans' studio doorstep was the Kemble Theatre in Broad Street. Until the construction of the Courtyard, it was Hereford's last live theatre. Claimed by the *Birmingham Post* to be one of the oldest in the country, the Kemble had billed such famous players as Sarah Siddons, John Kemble and David Garrick.

The technical difficulties of theatre photography with comparatively slow films and lenses
experienced by Derek Evans were recognised by no less than six awards for photographic
excellence in national and international exhibitions. This picture of an amateur operatic production
in Hereford was first hung at the 1950 London Annual Exhibition of The Royal Photographic
Society.

The Odeon cinema in High Town with the first of several films to show the sinking of the *Titanic*. Top billing was given to actor Kenneth Moore in *A Night to Remember*. Like the *Titanic*, the Odeon sank without trace leaving only an art-deco clock behind in the city museum.

Above and opposite: The seasons would bring annual 'diary' events and picture opportunities. From springtime crocus at the Bishop's Palace to street parties, the City Carnival and the Remembrance Day Parade.

Above and opposite: One of the floats which took part in the City Carnival in 1951 was a pirate ship, whose wayward crew took Miss Hereford and her escourts prisoner.

For centuries the Old Bridge was the only river crossing in the city for wheeled vehicles. Towards the end of the last century, buses and articulated lorries would cross it while pedestrians took refuge in the v-shaped buttresses. In January 1967 the new Greyfriars Bridge opened and took the strain.

Opposite: The Remembrance Day Parade at the War Memorial in St Peter's Square.

Above and opposite: All the glamour of the May Fair – although in the 1950s it was as much about titillation as white-knuckle rides. There was Glamour on Parade and The Gay Nineties all to be found in Commercial Road, along with Renetta the Strip-Tease Girl!

Today, the Health and Safety Executive might object (not to mention the Advertising Standards Authority), but in 1960 the May Fair could offer truly exciting and macabre possibilities.

Opposite: Television and radio comedian, Alfred Marks, left the world of show business annually to man the family's attraction at the May Fair.

Above: A heatwave in the summer of 1959 brought children flocking to the cool waters of the Wye.
Below: Some years later, a pool, strictly for model boats, and provided by Hereford Round Table,
succumbed to the warm weather and impatient toddlers.

STRICTLY
NO
PADDLING

A warm summer evening in 1958 and children are drawn to the Big Top of Bertram Mills' Circus. It's a high view of the photographer's youngest daughter, Diana, from a stilted programme seller.

And others almost stood to attention in awe.

Above and opposite: With so many elephants on show at the circus they had to arrive by train at Barrs Court station. Excitement mounted in town as most of the elephants walked tail-in-trunk to the Big Top, although one lucky elephant rode in a specially constructed jeep.

A veteran car rally, outside the Old Town House in High Town, in the August sunshine, 1959.

Opposite: Late in the summer (journalism's 'silly season') the studio stock of 'pretty-pretty' pictures would be replenished with views like this unchanging scene at Eardisland. This picture celebrated its win as Herefordshire's best-kept village in 1959; a title previously won in 1956.

And by the fading evening light a band from Whitecross School play to Christmas shoppers.

January, 1960 and the milkman struggles to deliver milk to a flooded Edgar Street ...

... while the Wye rages.

Above and following pages: Winter snows always brought new pictures as studio work ground to a halt.

Sunshine and snow on Castle Green.

Nelson's Column casts a shadow across Castle Green and its winter mantle. The monument was refurbished for the 2005 bi-centenary celebrations of the Battle of Trafalgar.

Waking to early snow ...

... and scurrying home through the Cathedral Close.

Steaming away from Hereford railway station.

two

But whatever the weather the city folk went on...

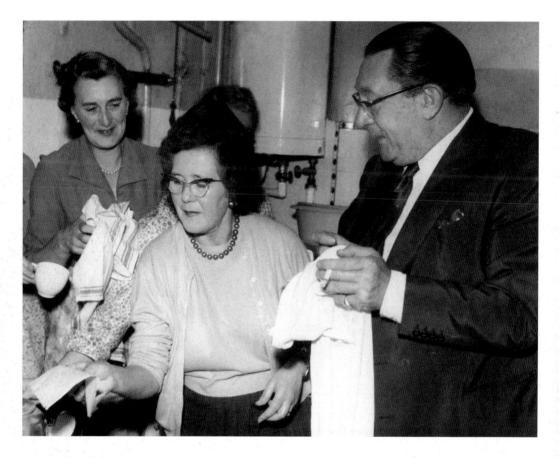

Above: In his day, Hereford-born television and radio personality, Gilbert Harding, was one of the most famous men in Britain. At the height of his fame in October, 1959 he helped wash up at the Langford House Christmas Fair at the Town Hall.

Opposite: Every year, staff at the old County Hospital held a Christmas party and traditionally the young nurses danced the can-can. The lucky photographer got to compere the show!

Following pages: In 1958, Frank Owen was the Liberal candidate in the Hereford by-election. The voice of Test Cricket BBC radio, and future television commentator, John Arlott, joined him to persuade farmers to support the Liberal cause.

Friends reunited … cricket and old school ties. Former England cricketer and Worcestershire captain Reg Perks emerged from the crowd to join John Arlott and Frank Owen. The celebrated cricketer was a former pupil of Hereford High School for boys and a childhood chum of the candidate.

Above: Campaigning and perhaps sure of his eventual success, Conservative candidate David (later Sir David) Gibson-Watt canvasses over a cup of strong tea ...

Opposite: ... while 'Supermac', Prime Minister Harold Macmillan, on a tour of marginal constituencies, wonders how to keep his candidate's mind on the job!

The campaign ended in a time-honoured way with a torchlight procession through the town.
Polling was light due to bad weather – snow fell during the day and a there was a sharp frost in
the evening.

Opposite: The Liberals were always sure of one vote. Eighty-eight-year-old Dan O'Neil had worked for Liberal candidates in nineteen general elections. A member of the party for seventy-five years he appreciated a kiss from Frank Owens's wife Grace – an American ex-actress.

Right and below: The Great TV Inquisitor. Robin (later Sir Robin) Day was adopted prospective Liberal parliamentary candidate for the South Hereford constituency in April, 1959. Planning the campaign from the Liberal Association rooms in Widemarsh Street, he took to the streets with loudhailer and snappy slogans.

These pages and following pages: Spin, Old Labour style, as supporters of candidate Brian Stanley took to the streets with sandwich boards. Despite all the efforts of other parties, the Conservatives were to securely hold the constituency until the election of Liberal Paul Keetch in 1997.

Others thought that no party had the answers. A dignified protest on the Cathedral Close by members of CND at the 1959 commemoration of the Battle of Britain.

Then aged sixty, William (Bill) Piggott, former Alderman and Mayor of Hereford led a homeless family into a condemned house challenging authorities to prosecute him 'if they dare'. Once through the window, he welcomed thirty-five-year-old ex-sailor Fred Newman, his twenty-year-old wife Phyllis and two children into No. 2 Wye Street. Local schoolmaster, Mr Gerry Pullen, stands by in support.

23 April may be St George's Day to most but to Mr and Mrs Cecil Clements of
Frederick Avenue it was the family birthday. Five years separated the youngest
and oldest of their three children but all of them were born on St George's Day,
and none of them was even named George. 'We didn't like the name,' said Mrs
Clements. 'When the first arrived we chose the name of the patron saint of Wales
instead'. David was born in 1945. Exactly a year later Carol followed, then four
years later Robert arrived, again on 23 April. The children were a musical trio
David played solo cornet in Hereford City Silver Band, Robert learnt the same
instrument, while Carol was a promising pianist. Birthday meant only one party
with one big cake – made by their father, a baker by trade.

Above and below: In 1957, whenever Pred Mark VII cruised the streets in its ten violent clashing colours heads turned. Jointly owned by Andrew Pyke, Colin Morris and David Prosser the 1934 Ford 8 was bought for £15. It carried a TV aerial, an 'air-brake' (an open umbrella) and hands painted in strategic positions imploring 'push'! On the back a sign said 'Don't laugh madam. Your daughter might be inside'.

In May 1956, an eighty-five-year-old woman made an archery range on former tennis courts at Ivy Lodge, Venns Lane. Miss Christine Anna Philips had for seventy years set aside an hour a day for archery practise and was hoping in her eighty-fifth year to compete in the Grand National Archery Competition.

Opposite: For two schoolboys the temptation of a quick peep was too much. In the doorway of Macdonald's newsagents, 'health and beauty' were proudly presented.

After twelve months' work, Master Wheelwright George Cox (top) and his only employee Albert Wood were ready to deliver yet another traditional gypsy caravan to a family in Somerset. In 1960, Mr Cox was the only man in Britain still making them. He expected that this particular one 'should last forty years'. Later in June the caravan was taken to Barrs Court station for its journey to Somerset. It was the first caravan of its type to be carried by rail for thirty-six years – the last also being made by the Hereford craftsman. Mr Cox would never discuss the cost of the caravans saying 'the gypsies wouldn't like it'. For a number of years caravans were returned to his Holmer Road home for refurbishment and repair. Mr Cox worked well into his eighties and lived to be over 100 years old.

Two magnificent shires being shod for retirement to a horses' home in Surrey in October, 1961. For ten years they had worked together pulling a brewery dray around the city streets. The experts at work are Mr Billy Watts Sr, a former Royal Show Champion Blacksmith and his son, also Billy. The smithy stood in Blue School Street and many are lucky enough to remember the sight, sound and smell of the forge, now covered by the Maylord Orchard's development,

The Hereford School of Farriery was sited at the junction of Newtown Road and Edgar Street, now the retail park of PC World and others. In 1960, apprentice blacksmiths, Dennis Barrett and Geoffrey Caines, took their final exams under the watchful eye of Mr William Watts.

The 'largest weekend catch since 1926' filled the shop of Brian (Fishy) Gardner with fresh Wye salmon in May, 1963. The fishmonger, on the corner of King Street and Bridge Street was offering whole fresh Wye salmon from 9s 6d each.

Never one to miss a chance to perform, artist Trevor Makinson borrowed wig and gown – and a mirror – to paint himself into the mural at the Green Man Inn, Fownhope.

Opposite: The artist painted at several other landmarks and here takes a momentary break from painting the mural in the ballroom of the now demolished Three Counties Hotel, which stood at the top of Aylestone Hill. The painting was some 88 square yards and a romantic interpretation of the artist's view of the Wye valley, bringing Raglan Castle and the cliffs of Chepstow onto the banks of the River Wye only a few fields away from the village of Hampton Bishop.

The late Bob Monkhouse plays to the camera while opening a butcher's shop in Commercial Road, Hereford. Nervously assisting him is Diana Day, who, over sixteen years and 183 shows, played Susan in the 1950s radio programme *The Clitheroe Kid*.

More seriously meaty, Polish-born Frank Taddy. Frank was the generous host of the Spread Eagle, who introduced Herefordians to the delights of the steak house. Sometimes a pedigree Hereford beast would be bought at a winter sale for the menu.

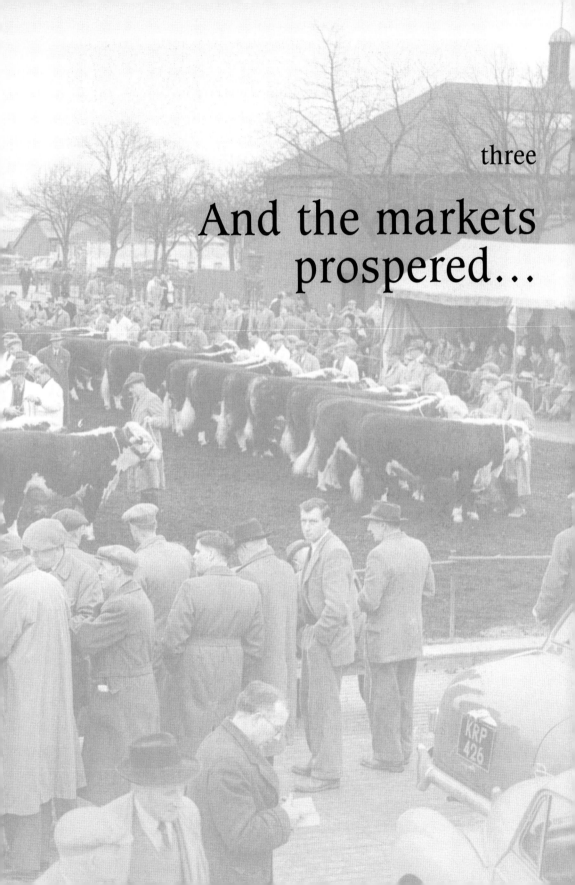

three

And the markets prospered...

A shaft of winter sunlight gave cathedral-like qualities to the Langford Sale Ring in January 1963. The picture graduated to that year's *Photography Year Book* – an annual collection of pictures judged to be the world's best.

Opposite above and below: The panic in the top photograph and the courage of an Olympic gold medallist meant this picture took up a half-page of the *Daily Express*, in October, 1959. The Annual Fayre Oaks Sale was well under way in Hereford cattle market when one pony dangerously reared up looking to escape through a gap in a wall of faces. From his front row seat, Col Harry Llewellyn (in the trilby hat), who had ridden his mount Foxhunter to Olympic Gold some years earlier, saved the day. Colonel Llewellyn would be photographed in Hereford again in April, 1964 when he officially opened The Foxhunter pub on Whitecross roundabout. In torrential rain in June, 1965 he was to be photographed burying the remains of Foxhunter in a cask on the Welsh Hills near his Abergavenny home.

Above: Two photographs of Shucknall Favourite, a Hereford 'aristocrat' from the world-famous Haven Herefords at Dilwyn, one of the greatest stock-getters of his time, retired to a 200-year-old cottage in January, 1958, donated by his owner Mr Leslie Lewis. Settled in, and at his leisure, he dictated the following poem to his benefactor and many admirers:

> The cottage you see in the photo beside
> Is mine, and I have it rent free
> For services rendered to Hereford cattle,
> Which are Hereford's main industry.
>
> The address is the Haven, an apt sort of name,
> So right when applying to me;
> For I'm now in retirement, next door to my Boss,
> Such friends and good neighbours are we.
>
> I'm proud of this job that I've done with this herd
> And I know Mr Lewis agrees,
> I've got him a stock with colour and bone
> Just right for the trade overseas.
>
> And though I am sorry to part with my wives
> I know that I must now I'm old,
> But I'm proud when I think of the prices obtained
> For my numerous family, when sold.
>
> And I'm proud of Vron Gaffer who takes on my job
> As perfect as type I've seen,
> He was Bull of the Year, and not only that,
> Was viewed by the Prince and the Queen.
>
> So if you are keen on cattle for beef,
> And the best of the Breed wish to see,
> Call in at the Haven, it's easy to find
> And I hope you will come and see me.

The house is now the charmingly restored home of Mr and Mrs J. Thomas who were the succeeding occupants.

And while Shucknall Favourite stayed home, others were paraded through the streets as proud symbols of their county.

The Hereford Herd Book Society drew buyers of the white-faced breed from all over the world.

One of the most famous and respected breeders of Hereford cattle, Captain R.S. deQuincey of the Vern, Marden, judging for the Supreme Champion of the Yard. Following his death in 1966, a then world-record price of £230,706 was paid for his Vern pedigree Hereford herd.

In December, 1955 *Country Life* magazine thought this a 'fashion note' for farmers.

The bustle of the market was only one side of rural life. The harvest was late in the Golden Valley, in 1956, producing this beautiful Vowchurch landscape.

Opposite: Sometimes there was a laugh to be had ...

Autumn brought the photographer's annual search for a ploughman. On this October, 1958 day Mr H. Samuel of Ledbury was the lone entrant in the horse-ploughing class of the Llanwarne and District Agricultural Improvement Society match at Hoarwithy.

Above and opposite: The first ever Englishman to win the Golden Plough Trophy as World Champion Ploughman. Twenty-seven-year-old Leslie Goodwin came back to his Dorstone farm in the Golden Valley in triumph in October, 1958. Trumpets sounded a fanfare in the city and church bells rang out across the Golden Valley. Holding aloft the Golden Plough, won in Stuttgart, the champion's arrival at Barrs Court railway station attracted cheering crowds before the celebrations moved to the Town Hall where the Mayor of Hereford, Cllr David Shaw hosted the reception.

Going up! Weightlifting at Michaelchurch Escley fête in July, 1959.

Coming down! Taking a tumble at the fête some years later. Ponies were rounded up from the surrounding hills and the attraction of a rodeo was added to the summer fête. Few stayed on their mounts for long and seldom did a rider make the centre of the ring!

Above and opposite: Once as unremarkable as a man with a mobile phone, these persistent figures from a rural past were in fact disappearing. Derek Evans was always watchful for characters and faces and potentially more Gold Medal winning exhibitions pictures.

Away from the hard work of farming Mr Derek Hackett of Bridstow, Ross-on-Wye, had a passion for old tractors and by 1958 had seventeen of the earliest surviving examples. Newspaper cuttings describe this one as an 18hp Ivel built in Biggleswade in 1903. Another example of this machine survives in the London Science Museum.

Opposite: The villagers of Eardisley have long memories. In February, 1959 – after a gap of five years – they celebrated Fox Supper at Tram Inn. The tradition dated back eighteen years to the wartime broadcasts of Nazi propagandist Lord Haw-Haw and his claim that country dwellers in England were reduced to eating foxes! In defiance the local butcher produced a recipe for a fox pie available to all at a celebration evening. To the call of the horn of huntsman John Preece, Mrs Phyllis Parker ceremonially brought the pie to the table. Former village butcher Arthur Wynne (pictured), a founder of the club and sole keeper of the recipe, tucks in under the horrified gaze of a fox that didn't escape the hunt.

This page and opposite: Every year in June, since 1876, members of Fownhope Hearts of Oak Friendly Society have held their annual Club Walk through the village. Carrying bunches of flowers on sticks they attend a special service at the village church and afterwards call on various people, including the local doctor. Some get footsore and weary but most find time for a rousing cheer and a cooling pint of ale.

Taking a well-earned rest following the Fownhope Hearts of Oak Friendly Society's annual Club Walk.

Opposite: Dr Godfrey Malkin, on the doorstep of his home and surgery at Mona House, greeted the band and villagers before dispensing cool drinks. When Dr Malkin retired in the early '60s the house was renamed the Rowans.

The procession marched through the heart of the village in the mid-summer sunshine.

Opposite: Smiles and good-hearted banter with friends and neighbours epitomised the spirit of the walk.

In 1955, one man had walked in every procession since the beginning. Eighty-eight-year-old Mr E. Fortescue Gange was there again telling five-year-old David Gilbert about the very first walks.

Opposite: Sales and uses could be found for any picture good enough to stand as an image in its own right. Published by *The Birmingham Mail* in 1958, this picture, taken at the Fownhope Flower Walk, was sufficiently acclaimed to appear in the 1959 edition of *The Photography Year Book* — a collection of the world's best photographs. Later, the hungry open-mouthed expression would attract the makers of Aero chocolate bar to include it in a national advertising campaign suggesting, 'and suddenly you feel like an Aero'.

Above and following pages: Even today many can recall hop-picking mornings. They were remembered for the weak sun rising, vapours of mist drifting over meadows and hedges and the distinctive chill in the dewy morning air. Here was the chance to photograph a changing industry and a fading way of life. It was the end of summer and the start of hop picking was fun for the children and extra cash for hardworking mums. They came from Birmingham, across the West Midlands and even south Wales and were all drawn, along with the gypsies, to Herefordshire's extensive hopyards. City hop-picking families brought to the farms by bus and lorry, camped daily in the fields, wet or fine, for two weeks or so, cooking on improvised fires. While mother 'scratted' city children explored the tall avenues of hops, marvelled at the

awesome shires pulling the drays and wondered about the gypsies who were kept – or stayed – at a distance. The hop yards are all now completely mechanised, reduced in acreage and empty of people and horses.

Earnings were measured by the bushel and drama surrounded the 'busheller', a figure of authority, who arrived at the crib with his clerk in train and assorted labourers. One held open the vast hopsack, others with their long poles unhooked the last stubborn bines. The clerk recorded the shouted measures and marked the picker's card. 'Light bushellers' were much appreciated but 'heavy bushellers' the cause of much muttering.

Above: Women take a tea break from hop-picking. *Below:* Bushels of hops were measured basket by basket and the pickers' efforts recorded ready for pay-day.

Above and following pages: Herefordshire's ladies prepared themselves for The Women's Institute's annual picnic, here at Berrington Hall, and waited for the chance to be singled out by the photographer as icons of the time.

A simple Box-Brownie was the digital-camera equivalent of the day and you needed a cupped hand to shield the viewfinder ...

... and sometimes there was an abundance of creative hat-fashions.

But grim reality intruded in the rural scene. This tragic fire in October, 1959 at Perrystone Court, How Caple, seriously damaged the main part of the 300-year-old building. The owner Lt Gen. Sir Sidney Clive was rescued from the fire but died on his way to hospital.

Opposite: Children play in the rubble of what had been the hutted camp at Foxley near Mansel Lacey. Built as an American wartime hospital it later became a resettlement camp for Polish refugees where families scattered all over Europe were reunited by the British Red Cross. By November, 1959 Hereford Housing Committee were desperate to rehouse families in more permanent accommodation. The *Empire News* and *Sunday Chronicle* reported, 'The camp is littered with the rubble of buildings demolished by the Council as they are vacated, to prevent reoccupation by squatters'.

Above and opposite: Warm and secure – part of a delightful series of pictures, taken in the late '50s, of deaf children at Wessington Court, Woolhope. The specialist school for deaf children was privately founded in the mid-Victorian mansion in 1944. It was soon to close shortly after these pictures were taken. Miss N. Simpson, deaf herself, was one of three dedicated teachers.

Opposite and above: In April, 1957 Queen Elizabeth II made a visit to Hereford, unveiling a plaque at the Town Hall to commemorate the occasion. After inspecting pedigree Herefords in the cattle market she was greeted at the north porch of the cathedral by the Dean of Hereford, the very Reverend Hedley Burrows. Also in the picture is Sir Richard Cotterell, the Lord Lieutenant.

Right and overleaf: While in May, 1959 Princess Alexandra took time to tour a crowded Castle Green, meeting Girl Guides and Brownies.

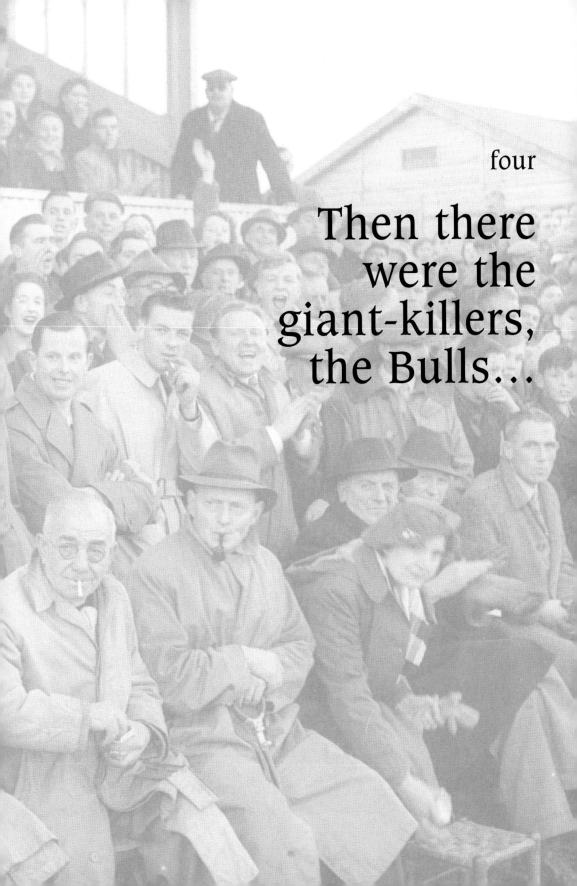

four

Then there were the giant-killers, the Bulls...

This page and opposite: Giving life–long support to Hereford United FC, brought its own rewards for the studio. Pictures on the pitch, supporters in trees, celebrations and the highs and lows of Southern League football.

Above and below: In December, 1956, the club faced an important FA Cup match. Members of the Supporters' Club volunteered to build additional terraces to accommodate an extra 2,000 spectators.

Cigar-smoking Len Weston, cider maker and then Chairman of Hereford United Football Club held a party at his Much Marcle home to celebrate the 1957 victory over Queen's Park Rangers. Gathered around the radio they listen to the third round draw of the FA Cup, which brought Sheffield Wednesday to Hereford. Pictured here, from left to right are: player-manager Joe Wade, with his wife Kay, his daughter Beverley and son Richard, Mrs Turner, club secretary Fred Turner, Len Weston, supporter Tommy Pugh and Mrs Weston.

Opposite above: For cider maker Len Weston, there was always an excuse or reason for merriment, with guests and workmen sharing equally.

Opposite below: The 1960 apple and perry-pear harvest was a record for the Weston family business at Much Marcle. As managing director of the firm Len said that his staff were working overtime and farmworkers were coming in for an evening's work in the factory after a day in the fields.

Right and below: A long association developed between the studio and cider makers HP Bulmer. Photographs of the plant, product and people were all featured. The giant oak vats in their underground cellarage in Ryeland Street (*right*) are now gone, covered over by the new housing development. Visiting pop group The Applejacks were soon immersed in the spirit of the cider-making season (*below*).

Former chairman of HP Bulmer, Bertram Bulmer, who epitomised the spirit of the developing company, tried his legs on a penny-farthing bicycle. Approaching his seventieth birthday he practised in the driveway of his home to prepare a novel way of starting a cycle race as part of the Herefordshire Cider Festival.

five

But the military held strong...

A hero of the time 'Monty' receives the adulation of service families and friends at Bradbury Lines. His October, 1942 victory against Rommel earned him the full title of Field Marshall the Viscount Montgomery of Alamein.

In a different world and time the brave young men of the SAS were sometimes the public face of Britain's armed forces. The team was preparing to fly to America to compete in the World's Free-Fall Parachuting competition.

November, 1956 and twenty-three geese were escorted by cooks, led by Sgt Bob Woodcock, across the square to the cookhouse at Bradbury Lines, home then to the Boys' Regiment, Royal Artillery. The geese were counted carefully because in 1955 the CO's pet goose failed

to escape the butcher's knife! The camp at Bradbury Lines later became the first home of the 22nd SAS regiment, from where its world-wide operations were launched.

January, 1960 and Meals on Wheels lead the relief operation for flooded villagers at Hampton Bishop.

February, 1956 and on a gun carriage drawn by boy soldiers of the Royal Artillery Boys' Regiment, Maj. Robert Cracknell left the army after nearly forty years' service. His army boots around his neck, he was hauled to the gates of Bradbury Lines and to a new life keeping poultry on civvy street.

six

And the church was always there...

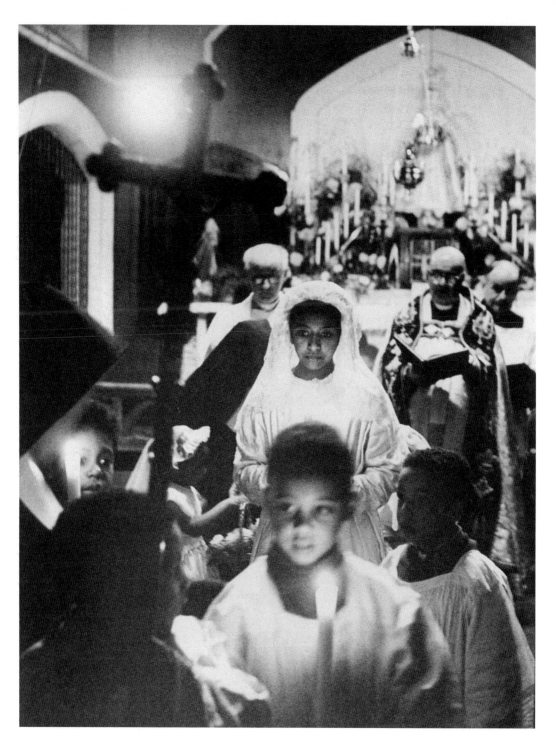

Shortly before Christmas, 1958, twenty-six-year-old Antonia Andrade became the first black woman to be admitted to the Order of the Poor Clares at Bullingham, under the name of Sister Mary Francis. The convent, now closed and demolished, was replaced with a new building at Much Birch.

Much-loved Catholic priest, who served generations of local families, Father (later Cannon) O'Connor watches closely as the ball rolls down the skittle alley at St Mary's presbytery fête.

Above and following pages: In 1947, Prebendary Leland Snell, Rural Dean of Hereford, started the animal service at Holy Trinity church, Whitecross Road. Reports at the time tell of lambs, and even heifers, being brought into the church with Pekinese sitting on pew rails and

ponies standing by the column of the nave. 'At one service,' said Marjory Scott, a former local RSPCA welfare centre committee member, 'we sang 'hallelujah!' twice. As we went to sing it a third time a duck quacked in perfect harmony. The hymn ended in loud laughter.'

This page and following pages: As kittens, bees, fowl and armfuls of puppies were brought to be blessed at Holy Trinity church, PC Roy Short, looking every inch the typical English 'bobby', found little to challenge the law of the land.

Duty done, one donkey, tied to the gate, just couldn't wait to get home.

More crowds … always crowds at Holy Trinity! Prebendary Leland Snell, Rural Dean of
Hereford, is seen among the crowd on the left in the picture.

Opposite: A less well-known image of the late colourful character Colin 'Boxer' Jones – kitten in
pocket in May, 1958 at the Holy Trinity Pets' Service. The picture was subsequently published in
The Photography Year Book, from 1958.

Like today the demolition men and builders came and went. At 5 o'clock on the morning of 10 July 1963, demolition men brought the Kemble Theatre pillars crashing to the Broad Street pavement marking the end of an epoch in theatrical history.

Opposite above: Little is known of this sea of smiling faces except an entry 'Sunday School outing, Holy Trinity, Whitecross' …

Opposite below: … but sometimes buses queued, in St Owen's Street, to take them all off on an outing.

A view across the city from the Quarry Road part of Tupsley. The boiler chimney, almost in line with the cathedral, served the steam sawmill of builder W. Bowers who was responsible for building Hereford Town Hall.

Left: Before the new Wye Bridge was constructed, the former terminal building of the Abergavenny to Hereford tramway stood almost opposite the Hereford Rowing Club. For many years, before it was demolished in 1958, it was known as Jordan's boatyard from where boats could be hired to idle away a few hours on the Wye.

Below: October, 1960 and shopkeepers in Ross-on-Wye were so indignant at the effect on Christmas trade, caused by the relaying of mains services, they petitioned the Minister of Transport, Ernie Marples, to postpone the work. The petition was refused.

seven

But sometimes there were animals...

'Give us a kiss'. The long-lost newspaper *The Empire News* and *Sunday Chronicle* of October, 1957 found space to publish this amusing picture of Champion Brutus and his new young friend.

Opposite: This puzzling pictorial 'stand-off' was featured in the *London Times*, 5 March 1959. Mr Robert Probert of Burghill had never before, in twenty years of farming, heard of such a strange adoption. These orphaned lambs were left in a pile of straw beside this heifer, who had lost her first calf five weeks before. An hour or two later, a stockman found her feeding the lambs.

While the approaching photographer lowers the camera to ground level, just a few feet away, a thrush bravely keeps watch over its dead mate. The picture was chosen by *The Times*, 6 May 1958 to illustrate The Royal Photographic Society's first photojournalism exhibition.

Opposite: Was seven-year-old Ginger, measuring 16 inches across the back, the Heaviest cat in England in September 1957? At 24lb he was certainly a handful for his owner Mrs E.M. Birch of The Hopton Arms, Munsley. Publication of this picture, both regionally and nationally, set the challenge, but 28lb Blackie from Cheshire won the day.

Then ten years old, Roger Bounds of Wallstyche Farm, Kington rode from his hillside home to school each day on Pansy, a fourteen-year-old pony. Where he stabled the horse at Kington Primary School is not known!

Opposite: A quick nip of the toe and an equally quick response from the photographer. On a Herefordshire farm in Spring, 1957, Tiger the lamb was only trying to make a friend of eleven-month-old Johnnie Gwilt.

A frequent visitor to Herefordshire, with his one-man circus, was Fred Able. He would sell you mice at 2s each and tell you of his TV appearance. If you didn't believe him he could show you the contract. His 7ft by 4ft wagon was neatly packed with fifty performing mice, fifteen rats, two dogs and a performing tumbler pigeon and was pulled by two donkeys. Naughty children were warned that if they did not behave they would be taken away by Fred Able!

Opposite: Summertime and the villagers of Bosbury were enjoying a Victorian-style game of cricket – even ferrying suitably attired villagers to the event by horse-drawn cart.

The photographer searched for that one last image and turning from the main event found this splendid 'Victorian policeman' at his ease.

A floodlit Hereford Cathedral, before the long-term restoration programme would cover it in scaffold.

Afterword

Well, that was then and this is now. Our imaginary roll of film – stretching, roughly, from the end of rationing with its echos of war-time to the emerging consumer economy of Prime Minister Harold Macmillan – went into the darkroom and emerged some fifty years later, onto a computer screen and into a world changed beyond belief. In the intervening fifty years or so, Herefordshire married Worcestershire and then got divorced. Landmarks came and mostly went. In the city, shopping developments overlaid medieval streets and pedestrianisation transformed High Town. In the countryside a slow exodus of farm workers began as mechanisation took hold. It needed a photographer of wit, instinct and intuition to record these changing times and Derek Evans's gifts certainly matched the period.

Other local titles published by Tempus

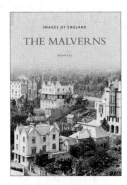

The Malverns
BRIAN ILES

This collection of over 200 archive photographs documents life in the Malverns from the 1860s until the 1950s. All aspects of everyday life are featured here, including shops and businesses, work and leisure and the war years. Local events such as the Bicycle Carnivals at Malvern Link are also recalled. *The Malverns* will delight those who want to know more about the history of the area.

0 7524 3667 8

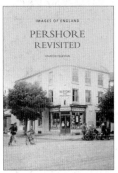

Pershore Revisited
MARION FREEMAN

This collection of over 200 archive photographs reveals some of the changes that have taken place in the Worcestershire town of Pershore over the last century. The Pershore Festival, Empire Day celebrations and the annual fair, fruit harvests and hop-picking are some of the local events featured here. This volume explores all aspects of everyday life, from shops and businesses to churches and schools.

0 7524 3737 2

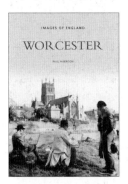

Worcester
PAUL HARRISON

All aspects of everyday life are recorded here, from shops and businesses, schools and hospitals, to pubs and hotels, work and leisure. Landmarks such as the city's eleventh-century cathedral, Lich Street and The Foregate, home to Worcester's Hop Market, are featured and events such as King George VI's coronation celebrations in 1937.

0 7524 3726 7

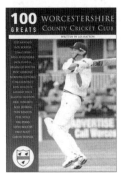

Worcestershire County Cricket Club 100 Greats
LES HATTON

Worcestershire celebrated 100 years of first-class cricket in 1999. The seven Foster brothers were members of the side during the early days, three of them appearing in the first Championship match at New Road against Yorkshire. Also, among these great Worcestershire cricketers are Ted Arnold, Albert Bird, Fred Bowley, Dick Burrows, Tom Straw, Fred Wheldon and George Wilson, all members of the team during that first 1899 season.

0 7524 2415 7

If you are interested in purchasing other books published by Tempus, or in case you have difficulty finding any Tempus books in your local bookshop, you can also place orders directly through our website

www.tempus-publishing.com